An

by Iain Gray

WRITING *to* REMEMBER

79 Main Street, Newtongrange,
Midlothian EH22 4NA
Tel: 0131 344 0414   Fax: 0845 075 6085
E-mail: info@lang-syne.co.uk
www.langsyneshop.co.uk

Design by Dorothy Meikle
Printed by Ricoh Print Scotland
© Lang Syne Publishers Ltd 2014

All rights reserved. No part of this publication may be reproduced, stored
or introduced into a retrieval system, or transmitted in any form or by any
means (electronic, mechanical, photocopying, recording or otherwise) without
the prior written permission of Lang Syne Publishers Ltd.

ISBN 978-1-85217-580-1

Anderson

MOTTO:
Stand sure.

CREST:
An oak tree.

NAME variations include:
Andersen
Andersonne
Andersson
Andersoun
Andresen
Andrewson

Chapter one:

The origins of popular surnames

by George Forbes and Iain Gray

If you don't know where you came from, you won't know where you're going **is a frequently quoted observation and one that has a particular resonance today when there has been a marked upsurge in interest in genealogy, with increasing numbers of people curious to trace their family roots.**

Main sources for genealogical research include census returns and official records of births, marriages and deaths – and the key to unlocking the detail they contain is obviously a family surname, one that has been 'inherited' and passed from generation to generation.

No matter our station in life, we all have a surname – but it was not until about the middle of the fourteenth century that the practice of being identified by a particular surname became commonly established throughout the British Isles.

Previous to this, it was normal for a person to be identified through the use of only a forename.

But as population gradually increased and there were many more people with the same forename, surnames were adopted to distinguish one person, or community, from another.

Many common English surnames are patronymic in origin, meaning they stem from the forename of one's father – with 'Johnson,' for example, indicating 'son of John.'

It was the Normans, in the wake of their eleventh century conquest of Anglo-Saxon England, a pivotal moment in the nation's history, who first brought surnames into usage – although it was a gradual process.

For the Normans, these were names initially based on the title of their estates, local villages and chateaux in France to distinguish and identify these landholdings.

Such grand descriptions also helped enhance the prestige of these warlords and generally glorify their lofty positions high above the humble serfs slaving away below in the pecking order who had only single names, often with Biblical connotations as in Pierre and Jacques.

The only descriptive distinctions among the peasantry concerned their occupations, like 'Pierre the swineherd' or 'Jacques the ferryman.'

Roots of surnames that came into usage in England not only included Norman-French, but also Old French, Old Norse, Old English, Middle English, German, Latin, Greek, Hebrew and the Gaelic languages of the Celts.

The Normans themselves were originally Vikings, or 'Northmen', who raided, colonised and eventually settled down around the French coastline.

The had sailed up the Seine in their longboats in 900AD under their ferocious leader Rollo and ruled the roost in north eastern France before sailing over to conquer England in 1066 under Duke William of Normandy – better known to posterity as William the Conqueror, or King William I of England.

Granted lands in the newly-conquered England, some of their descendants later acquired territories in Wales, Scotland and Ireland – taking not only their own surnames, but also the practice of adopting a surname, with them.

But it was in England where Norman rule and custom first impacted, particularly in relation to the adoption of surnames.

This is reflected in the famous *Domesday Book*, a massive survey of much of England and Wales, ordered by William I, to determine who owned what, what it was worth and therefore how much they were liable to pay in taxes to the voracious Royal Exchequer.

Completed in 1086 and now held in the National Archives in Kew, London, 'Domesday' was an Old English word meaning 'Day of Judgement.'

This was because, in the words of one contemporary chronicler, "its decisions, like those of the Last Judgement, are unalterable."

It had been a requirement of all those English landholders – from the richest to the poorest – that they identify themselves for the purposes of the survey and for future reference by means of a surname.

This is why the *Domesday Book*, although written in Latin as was the practice for several centuries with both civic and ecclesiastical records, is an invaluable source for the early appearance of a wide range of English surnames.

Several of these names were coined in connection with occupations.

These include Baker and Smith, while Cooks, Chamberlains, Constables and Porters were to be found carrying out duties in large medieval households.

The church's influence can be found in names such as Bishop, Friar and Monk while the popular name of Bennett derives from the late fifth to mid-sixth century Saint Benedict, founder of the Benedictine order of monks.

The early medical profession is represented by Barber, while businessmen produced names that include Merchant and Sellers.

Down at the village watermill, the names that cropped up included Millar/Miller, Walker and Fuller, while other self-explanatory trades included Cooper, Tailor, Mason and Wright.

Even the scenery was utilised as in Moor, Hill, Wood and Forrest – while the hunt and the chase supplied names that include Hunter, Falconer, Fowler and Fox.

Colours are also a source of popular surnames, as in Black, Brown, Gray/Grey, Green and White, and would have denoted the colour of the clothing the person habitually wore or, apart from the obvious exception of 'Green', one's hair colouring or even complexion.

The surname Red developed into Reid, while

Blue was rare and no-one wanted to be associated with yellow.

Rather self-important individuals took surnames that include Goodman and Wiseman, while physical attributes crept into surnames such as Small and Little.

Many families proudly boast the heraldic device known as a Coat of Arms, as featured on our front cover.

The central motif of the Coat of Arms would originally have been what was borne on the shield of a warrior to distinguish himself from others on the battlefield.

Not featured on the Coat of Arms, but highlighted on page three, is the family motto and related crest – with the latter frequently different from the central motif.

Adding further variety to the rich cultural heritage that is represented by surnames is the appearance in recent times in lists of the 100 most common names found in England of ones that include Khan, Patel and Singh – names that have proud roots in the vast sub-continent of India.

Echoes of a far distant past can still be found in our surnames and they can be borne with pride in commemoration of our forebears.

Chapter two:

Honours and distinction

A surname derived from the popular given name of 'Andrew', in turn derived from the Greek 'Andreas', indicating 'manly', 'Anderson' has a number of points of origin.

With the Scottish-Gaelic derivation of 'Gilleaindreas', or 'MacGhillieAndrais', it denotes 'servant of St Andrew' Scotland's patron saint, while from earliest times it also simply denoted 'son of Andrew.'

A name not confined to any particular country, Scandinavian forms include 'Andersen' and 'Andersson', with the former also found throughout the British Isles.

While the name in Scotland, also in the form of 'Gillanders', was from about the thirteenth century identified with the Badenoch area – to where a family of bearers of the name are believed to have moved from Moidart – the earliest record of the name, in the form of 'Andreu', is recorded in 1237 in the English county of Buckinghamshire.

This record relates to a William Andreu, and

the fact that his name appears on record indicates that he would have been a person of some importance or substance.

Although 'Anderson', in this case in the now redundant spelling variant of 'Andreu', appears on record more than 170 years after the adoption of surnames was popularised in the wake of the Norman Conquest, the ancestors of bearers of what would become the surname were present on English shores for a considerable period before the Conquest.

This means that flowing through the veins of many bearers of the name today may well be the blood of those Germanic tribes who invaded and settled in the south and east of the island of Britain from about the early fifth century.

Known as the Anglo-Saxons, they were composed of the Jutes, from the area of the Jutland Peninsula in modern Denmark, the Saxons from Lower Saxony, in modern Germany and the Angles from the Angeln area of Germany.

It was the Angles who gave the name 'Engla land', or 'Aengla land' – better known as 'England.'

They held sway in what became known as England from approximately 550 until the Norman Conquest of 1066 – when Harold II, the last of the

Anglo-Saxon kings, was killed at the battle of Hastings by a mighty force led by Duke William of Normandy.

William was declared King of England on December 25, and the complete subjugation of his Anglo-Saxon subjects followed.

Those Normans who had fought on his behalf were rewarded with the lands of Anglo-Saxons, many of whom sought exile abroad as mercenaries.

Within an astonishingly short space of time, Norman manners, customs and law were imposed on England – laying the basis for what subsequently became established 'English' custom and practice.

But beneath the surface, old Anglo-Saxon culture was not totally eradicated, with some aspects absorbed into those of the Normans, while faint echoes of the Anglo-Saxon past is still seen today in the form of popular surnames such as Anderson.

Bearers of the name came to feature in the pages of the high drama that is England's frequently turbulent history.

Born in Newcastle in 1582, Sir Henry Anderson was the prominent politician who supported the Royalist cause during the bitter English Civil War.

The monarch Charles I had incurred the

wrath of Parliament by his insistence on the 'divine right' of monarchs, and added to this was Parliament's fear of Catholic 'subversion' against the state and the king's stubborn refusal to grant demands for religious and constitutional concessions.

Matters came to a head with the outbreak of the civil war in 1642, with Parliamentary forces, known as the New Model Army and commanded by Oliver Cromwell and Sir Thomas Fairfax, arrayed against the Royalist army of the king.

In what became an increasingly bloody and complex conflict, spreading to Scotland and Ireland and with rapidly shifting loyalties on both sides, the 49-year-old king was eventually captured and executed in January of 1649 on the orders of Parliament.

Anderson, meanwhile, who had graduated from Christ College, Oxford, was knighted in 1608 and elected mayor of Newcastle in 1613. A year later, he was elected Member of Parliament (MP) for Newcastle upon Tyne and later as High Sheriff of Northumberland.

Re-elected as an MP on five occasions, up until 1640 – two years before the outbreak of the civil war – he was punished by being ousted from what was known as the Long Parliament for his support of the ill-fated Charles I.

An indication of the high honours and distinction that the Andersons have gained over the centuries is that a number of baronetcies have been created for bearers of the name – a baronetcy being an honour first granted in England in the early 1300s.

They include the Anderson Baronetcy of St Ives, in the County of Huntingdon, created in the Baronetage of England in 1629 for John Anderson; the Baronetcy of Penley, in the County of Hertford, was created in the Baronetage of England in 1643 for Henry Anderson, while the Baronetcy of Broughton, in the County of Lincoln, was created in the Baronetage of England in 1660 for Edmund Anderson.

Also in the Baronetage of England, the Baronetcy of Eyworth, in the County of Bedford, was created in 1664 for Stephen Anderson.

In the Baronetage of Great Britain, the Baronetcy of Mill Hill, Hendon, in the County of Middlesex, was created in 1798 for John Anderson, who served as Lord Mayor of London from 1797 to 1798.

A number of baronetcies in the Baronetage of the United Kingdom have also been created, with the

Baronetcy of Fermoy, in the County of Cork, created in 1813 for James Anderson and the Baronetcy of Parkmount, in the County of the City of Belfast and of Mullaghmore in the County of Monaghan, created in 1911 for Robert Anderson, who served as Lord Mayor of Belfast from 1908 to 1910.

Also in the Baronetage of the United Kingdom, the Baronetcy of Ardtaraig, in the County of Perth, was created in 1919 for the Scottish public servant and businessman Kenneth Anderson, while the Baronetcy of Harrold Priory, in the County of Bedford, was created in 1920 for the Scots-born writer, lecturer and businessman John Anderson.

All these baronetcies, granted on a hereditary basis, fell into extinction after the last holders of the title died without succession.

A more recent baronetcy, granted on the basis of a life peerage, is that of Baron Anderson of Swansea, in the County of West Glamorgan, created in 2005 for the former Labour MP Donald Anderson.

Born in Swansea in 1939, he served as MP for Monmouth from 1966 to 1970 and Swansea East from 1974 to 2005 – making him one of the longest serving MPs in recent years.

A number of Coats of Arms have been

granted to English bearers of the Anderson name and it is one of these that is featured on the front cover of this booklet.

The Crest and Motto featured on page three are those of the Scottish Clan Anderson – with whom many of the name, regardless of nationality, have an affinity.

Chapter three:

Inquiring minds

Bearers of the name have stamped their mark on the historical record through a rich variety of endeavours and pursuits.

Known for his association with Freemasonry, James Anderson was the Scottish minister and writer born in 1679 in Aberdeen.

Ordained a Church of Scotland minister in 1707, he later settled in London and ministered to a number of congregations that included the Presbyterian Church in Swallow Street, the Lisle Street Chapel and the Glass House Street congregation.

It was in 1721, when Freemasonry was undergoing a great revival throughout the United Kingdom, Europe and North America, that its ruling English body, the Grand Lodge, charged Anderson, who was Master of a Masonic lodge and a Grand Master of the Grand Lodge in London and Westminster, to produce a definitive digest of the ancient craft's institutions.

This authoritative work was first published in 1723 as *The Constitutions of the Free-Masons* – more popularly known as *Anderson's Constitutions* – while, before his death in 1739 he also wrote a number of other works that include *A Defence of Masonry*.

Born in Aberdeen in 1582, Alexander Anderson was the mathematician who made a significant contribution to the study of both algebra and geometrical analysis.

Very little is known about his early life, but he first came to notice in Paris – where he in all probability had gone to study – publishing mathematical tracts between 1612 and 1619, the year of his death.

He was related to David Anderson of Finshaugh, Aberdeen, known as "Davie Do-a'-things" because of his mathematical and inventive genius – with one of his many renowned feats figuring out how to successfully remove a large rock that had obstructed the entrance to Aberdeen harbour.

One of his grandsons, meanwhile, was the mathematician James Gregory, who in 1663 published a treatise describing a design for a reflecting telescope.

One colourful bearer of the name was John Anderson, born in Rosneath, Dunbartonshire in 1726 and who went on to hold the prestigious post of professor of natural philosophy – as the study of physics was then known – at Glasgow University.

Despite his highly volatile nature, he appears to have been adored by his students – and one clue to his highly complex temperament can be found in the nickname bestowed on him by these students of 'Jolly Jack Phosphorous.'

This was a nickname that referred to not only his truly explosive experiments and inventions in the realms of experimental physics, but also to his explosive nature and rigid Evangelical Christian beliefs.

In 1786, 'Jolly Jack' published a groundbreaking textbook on physics that subsequently ran through another four editions. It was in recognition of this that the scientific 'think-tank' known as the Royal Society elected him to its elite ranks.

He was also a friend of not only the Scottish engineer and inventor James Watt – having asked Watt to repair a steam engine for him – but also of the American statesman, fellow Royal Society member and inventor Benjamin Franklin.

He died in 1796, leaving the bulk of his estate for the foundation of a new institution of learning in Glasgow, one in which emphasis would be placed on the provision of a practical education for both men and women from ordinary backgrounds

At first located in Glasgow's John Street and later in George Street, the new institution opened its doors only a few years after its benefactor's death, and was at first known as Anderson's College.

The institution went through several changes in both structure and name until it received its Royal Charter in 1964 as Strathclyde University, now the third largest university in Scotland.

Also in the sciences, Carl Anderson, born in New York City in 1905 and who died in 1991, was the American physicist who won the 1936 Nobel Prize in Physics, along with Victor Hess, for their discovery of the positron – the 'anti-matter' counterpart of the electron.

Yet another particularly accomplished bearer of the Anderson name was Elizabeth Garrett Anderson, whose many 'firsts' include the first Englishwoman to qualify as a physician and surgeon in Britain.

Born in 1836 in Whitechapel, London, the second of eleven children, she moved as a child with her family to Snape, Sussex, where her father bought a barley and coal merchant business.

Receiving her early education from her

mother and later a governess, it was not until she was aged 13 that she was sent to a private boarding school in London.

Later becoming a friend of Emily Davies, the early feminist and co-founder of Girton College, Cambridge, she determined on a career in medicine and, accordingly, in 1860 she studied to become a surgery nurse at Middlesex Hospital, London.

This was at a time when the career of physician was effectively barred to women, but by dint of her dogged determination and through private study with the Society of Apothecaries, in 1865 she passed its examination and was licensed to practise medicine – making her the first woman in Britain to do so.

Opening her own practice in Upper Berkeley Street, London, she also later obtained a medical degree from the University of Sorbonne, Paris, while in 1870 she was appointed one of the visiting physicians of the East London Hospital for Children.

Co-founder of the London School of Medicine for Women and dean of the institution from 1883 to 1902, she also became the first female mayor in London when, in 1908, she was elected mayor of Aldeburgh.

Also active in the women's suffrage movement, she died in 1917, while a year after her death the hospital she co-founded was renamed the Elizabeth Garrett Anderson Hospital in her honour.

The hospital was amalgamated in 2001 with the Obstetric Hospital to become the Elizabeth Garrett Anderson and Obstetric Hospital and, after relocating, is now the Elizabeth Garrett Anderson wing at University College Hospital.

On foreign shores, Anton Anderson, born in 1892 in Moonlight, New Zealand, to a Swedish father and an Irish mother and moving at the age of 22 to the United States to work as a surveyor, became known as "Mr Alaska Railroad."

Obtaining a degree in engineering from Seattle University, he moved to Anchorage, Alaska, to work for the Alaskan Engineering Commission – and as its chief engineer was instrumental in the construction of the Alaska Railroad.

Mayor of Anchorage from 1956 to 1958 and a president of the American Society of Engineers, he died in 1960, while the Anton Anderson Memorial Tunnel from Whittier to Portage, Alaska, is named in his honour.

One particularly infamous bearer of the

otherwise proud name of Anderson was William T. Anderson, better known to posterity as "Bloody Bill."

Born in 1840 in Hopkins County, Kentucky, he earned his unenviable nickname while fighting for the Confederate cause during the American Civil War of 1861 to 1865.

Joining the murderous Confederate guerrilla band known as Quantrill's Raiders in 1863, many of the atrocities carried out by the feared group include the Centralia Massacre.

This was in September of 1864 when they captured a passenger train near Centralia, Missouri and killed 24 Union soldiers who had also been aboard and, later that same day, killing more than 100 Union militiamen in an ambush.

"Bloody Bill" was himself killed a month later.

Chapter four:

On the world stage

Of English, Irish and German descent, Gillian Anderson is the American actress best known for her role of FBI Special Agent Dana Scully in *The X-Files* television series.

Born in Chicago in 1968, it was after her birth that her mother, a computer analyst, and her father, owner of a film post-production company, moved to Puerto Rico for a brief period before settling in the United Kingdom. Aged 11, Anderson and her parents moved back to the United States, settling in Grand Rapids, Michigan.

Her stage career began after she moved to New York and had a role in the Alan Ayckbourn play *Absent Friends* at the Manhattan Theatre Club, winning the 1990-1991 Theatre World Newcomer Award.

She was later cast as Special Agent Scully in *The X-Files*, a series that ran for nine seasons and for which she won a number of awards including an Emmy and a Golden Globe, while she also starred in the 1998 feature film *The X-Files* and the 2008 *The X-Files (I Want to Believe)*.

Other film credits include the 2000 *The House of Mirth* and the 2006 *The Last King of Scotland*, while to great critical acclaim she played the role of Miss Haversham in a 2011 BBC adaptation of *Great Expectations*, and also featured in the 2013 BBC Two and RTÉ One drama serial *The Fall*.

Born in Adelaide in 1897, Francis Margaret Anderson was the Australian actress of stage, film and television better known as Judith Anderson and, later, as **Dame Judith Anderson**.

Settling in the United States, she became established as a leading Broadway actress in the 1930s and continued her stage career throughout the following two decades.

Stage credits include the playwright Eugene O'Neill's *Mourning Becomes Electra* and a 1936 production of *Hamlet*, while film credits include the 1940 *Rebecca*, for which she was nominated for an Academy Award for Best Supporting Actress.

Created a Dame Commander of the Order of the British Empire (DBE) in 1960, she was also named a Companion of the Order of Australia a year before her death in 1992 in recognition of her service to the performing arts.

Born in 1970, **Anthony Anderson** is the

American actor who, in addition to roles in television dramas that include *The Shield* and *Law & Order*, has also starred in his own sitcom, *The Andersons*.

A Scottish actress of stage, film and television, **Rona Anderson** was born in Edinburgh in 1926. Married to the late Scottish actor Gordon Jackson and with film credits that include the 1969 *The Prime of Miss Jean Brodie*, she died in 2013.

Best known, along with his wife Sylvia Anderson, for futuristic television series that include *Fireball XL5*, *Thunderbirds*, *Stingray*, *Captain Scarlet and the Mysterons* and *Space: 1999*, Gerald Alexander Abrahams, born in 1929 in Bloomsbury, London, was the English television and film producer and director better known as **Gerry Anderson**.

A pioneer of productions filmed in Supermarionation – involving the use of marionette puppets – and the recipient of an MBE, he died in 2012.

Actress, playwright, screenwriter and director, **Jane Anderson** was born in 1954 in New Jersey. Writer and director of the 2005 film *The Prize*, she was nominated for the 2009 Writers Guild of America Award for Best Dramatic Series for her work on television's *Mad Men*.

Winner of both the Top Entertainment Presenter and the Top Radio Comedy Personality awards at the 1991 British Comedy Awards, **Clive Anderson** is the radio and television presenter and author born in 1952 in Middlesex.

A former barrister, he is best known as host of the television show *Whose Line is it Anyway?* and the chat shows *Clive Anderson Talks Back* and *Clive Anderson all Talk*.

Bearers of the Anderson name have also excelled in the highly competitive world of sport.

On the fields of European football, **Russell Anderson**, born in Aberdeen in 1978, is the Scottish centre back who has played for teams that include Aberdeen and Sunderland.

The recipient of an MBE, Vivian Anderson, better known as **Viv Anderson**, born in 1956 in Clifton, Nottingham, is the English former defender noted for being the first black footballer to represent England in a full international match.

This was in 1978, while teams he played for include Manchester United, Nottingham Forest, Arsenal and Sheffield Wednesday.

From the football pitch to the cricket pitch, James Anderson, better known as **Jimmy Anderson**, is the English fast pace bowler who has represented his country in more than 80 Test Matches and more than 160 One Day Internationals.

Born in 1982 in Burnley, Lancashire, and playing first-class cricket for Lancashire, at the time of writing he is only the fourth English bowler to take 300 Test wickets.

On the dart board, **Gary Anderson** is the Scottish professional player nicknamed "The Flying Scotsman." Born in 1970 in Eyemouth, in the Borders, he won the 2007 World Darts Trophy and the Premier League title in 2011.

In the creative world of music, **Ian Anderson** is the Scottish singer, songwriter and multi-instrumentalist best known as the front-man of the band Jethro Tull.

Born in 1947 in Dunfermline but later moving with his family south of the border to Blackpool, Lancashire, he has enjoyed international success with singles that include the 1969 *Living in the Past* and albums that include *Benefit*, *Aqualung*, *Thick as a Brick*, *Songs from the Wood* and *Under Wraps*.

Also a successful solo artist with albums that include *The Secret Language of Birds*, he is the recipient of a number of honours and awards for his musical accomplishments that include a MBE, the 2006 Ivor Novello Award for International Achievement and the Prog God award at the 2013 Progressive Music Awards.

Still in the world of progressive music, John Roy Anderson, better known as **Jon Anderson** is the singer, songwriter and multi-instrumentalist best known as the former lead vocalist of the band Yes.

Born in 1944 in Accrington, Lancashire, he enjoyed hit albums with Yes that include the 1969 *Yes* and the 1970 *Time and a Word*.

From progressive music to country music, **Liz Anderson**, born Elizabeth Jane Haaby in Roseau, Minnesota, in 1930 and who died in 2011, was the singer and songwriter whose many awards include a Grammy in 1967 for Best Female Country Vocal Performance for her hit single *Mama Spank* and, along with Norman Jean and Bobby Bare, a nomination for Best Country Vocal – Group for their single *The Game of Triangles*.

Married to fellow songwriter Casey Anderson, she was the mother of the multi-award winning country music singer **Lynn Anderson**.

Born in 1947 in Grand Forks, Dakota, her

many hits include *Rose Garden*, while her awards include the 1974 American Music Award and Billboard Magazine's Female Artist of the Decade (1970-1980).

Born in 1945 in Houston, Renfrewshire, **Miller Anderson** is the Scottish blues guitarist and singer who has collaborated with bands that include the Keef Hartley Band, the Spencer Davis Group, Savoy Brown, Chicken Shack and T. Rex and others who include Maggie Bell, Zoot Money and the British Blues Quintet.

In a different music genre, **Moira Anderson** is the Scottish singer who, in addition to being known for her many appearances on the popular former television show *The White Heather Club*, was also host of her own equally popular show in 1968, *Moira Anderson Sings*.

Born in 1938 in Kirkintilloch, East Dunbartonshire, she was the recipient of an OBE in 1970 for her services to music.

Bearing a popular Scandinavian variant of the Anderson name, Göran Bror Andersson is the Swedish musician and composer better known as **Benny Andersson**, a founder member of the pop group ABBA.

Born in Stockholm in 1940, it was along with fellow composer Björn Ulvaeus, Anni-Frid Lynstad and Agnetha Fältskog, that he enjoyed a string of memorable international hits from 1972 to 1982 with songs that include *Waterloo*, winner for Sweden in 1974 of the Eurovision Song Contest.

From music to literature and with another variant of the Anderson name, **Hans Christian Andersen**, born in Odense, Denmark, in 1805, was the poet and author best known for his tales for children that include *The Ugly Duckling*, *Thumbelina* and *The Emperor's New Clothes*.

He died in 1875, while April 2, his birthday, is recognised as International Children's Book Day.

One particularly colourful bearer of the Anderson name was the Scottish stage magician **John Henry Anderson**, born in 1814, the son of a tenant farmer from Craigmyle, in the Mearns, about twenty miles from Aberdeen.

Orphaned at the age of ten, Anderson was apprenticed to a blacksmith, but by the time he was aged seventeen, enthralled by magic and illusion, he was performing on stage as The Great Caledonian Conjuror.

Although not the originator of the illusion,

his most popular act was the 'Gun Trick', or 'Bullet Catch Illusion', where he seemingly caught a bullet fired at him from a musket, while he is credited with the rather less dangerous trick of pulling rabbits from a hat.

By 1840, billing himself as The Great Wizard of the North, he embarked on a highly successful series of international tours, including the court of the Russian Tsar and throughout America.

Financial disaster struck when his Glasgow City Theatre, located on Glasgow Green was burned to the ground in an accident only a few weeks after it opened, leaving him bankrupt.

He attempted to recoup his fortunes with a further series of tours, but he suffered a number of setbacks and was near-destitute when he died in 1874.

By coincidence, this was also the year in which the legendary American illusionist and escapologist Harry Houdini was born, and at the height of his international fame he would cite Anderson as one of his main inspirations.

It was in tribute to Anderson that in 1909 Houdini arranged for the upkeep of his gravesite in Aberdeen's St Nicholas Churchyard after it had fallen into disrepair.